Primary Geography

Teacher's Book 3 Investigation

Stephen Scoffham | Colin Bridge

Geography in the primary school

Geography is the study of the Earth's surface. It helps children understand the human and physical forces which shape the environment. Children are naturally interested in their immediate surroundings. They also want to know about places beyond their direct experience. Geography is uniquely placed to satisfy this curiosity.

Geographical enquiries

Geography is an enquiry-led subject that seeks to answer fundamental questions such as:

- Where is this place?
- What is this place like (and why)?
- How and why is it changing?
- How does this place compare with other places?
- How and why are places connected?

These questions involve not only finding out about the natural processes which have shaped our environment, they also involve finding out how people have responded to them. Studying this interaction at a range of scales from the local to the global and asking questions about what is happening in the world around us lie at the heart of both academic and school geography.

Geographical perspectives

Geographical perspectives offer a uniquely powerful way of seeing the world. Since the time of the Ancient Greeks geographers have been attempting to chronicle and interpret their surroundings. One way of seeing links and connections is to think in terms of key ideas. Three concepts which geographers have found particularly useful in a range of settings are place, space and scale.

- Place focuses attention on the environment.
- Space focuses attention on location.
- Scale introduces a change in perspective that enables us to link the local and the global.

A layer of secondary concepts such as patterns, change and movement lie beneath these fundamental organising ideas and provide a way of further enhancing our understanding.

As they conduct their enquiries and investigations geographers make use of a number of specific skills. Foremost among these are mapwork and the ability to represent spatial information. The use of maps, charts, diagrams, tables, sketches and other cartographic techniques come under the more general heading of 'graphicacy' and are a distinguishing feature of geographical thinking. As more and more information has come to be represented electronically, the use of computers and other electronic applications has been championed by geography educators.

Geography in primary schools offers children from the earliest ages a fascinating window onto the contemporary world. The challenge for educators is to find ways of providing experiences and selecting content that will help children develop an increasingly deep understanding.

Collins Primary Geography

Collins Primary Geography is a complete programme for pupils in the primary school and can be used as a structure for teaching geography from ages 5-11. It consists of five pupil books and supporting teacher's guides with notes and copymasters. There is one pupil book at Key Stage 1 and four pupil books at Key Stage 2. There is also a supporting DVD for each Key Stage.

Aims

The overall aim of the programme is to inspire children with an enthusiasm for geography and to empower them as learners. The underlying principles include a commitment to international understanding in a more equitable world, a concern for the future welfare of the planet and a recognition that creativity, hope and optimism play a fundamental role in lasting learning. Three different dimensions – connecting to the environment, connecting to each other and connecting to ourselves – are explored throughout the programme in different contexts and at a range of scales. We believe that learning to think geographically in the broadest meaning of the term will help children make wise decisions in the future as they grow into adulthood.

Structure

Collins Primary Geography provides full coverage of the English National Curriculum requirements. Each pupil book covers a balanced range of themes and topics and includes case studies with a more precise focus:

- Book 1 and 2 *World around us* introduces pupils to the world at both a local and global scale.
- Book 3 *Investigation* encourages pupils to conduct their own research and enquiries.
- Book 4 *Movement* considers how movement affects the physical and human environment.
- Book 5 *Change* includes case studies on how places alter and develop.
- Book 6 *Issues* introduces more complex ideas to do with the environment and sustainability.

Although the books are not limited to a specific year band, Book 3 will be particularly suitable for Year 3 children. Similarly, Book 4 is focused on Year 4 children. However it is also possible to trace themes from one book to another. The programme is structured in such a way that key themes are revisited making it possible to investigate a specific topic in greater depth if required.

Investigations

Enquiries and investigations are an important part of pupils' work in primary geography. Asking questions and searching for answers can help children develop key knowledge, understanding and skills. Fieldwork is time consuming when it involves travelling to distant locations, but local area work can be equally effective. Many of the exercises in Collins Primary Geography focus on the classroom, school building and local environment. We believe that such activities can have a seminal role in promoting long term positive attitudes towards sustainability and the environment.

Places, themes and skills

Each book is divided into ten units giving a balance between places, themes and skills.

Places

There are locality studies throughout each book and studies of specific places from the UK, Europe and other continents. These studies illustrate how people interact with their physical surroundings in a constantly changing world. The places have been selected so that by the end of the scheme, children will be familiar with a balanced range of reference points from around the world. They should also have developed an increasingly sophisticated locational framework which will enable them to place their new knowledge in context.

Themes

Physical geography is covered in the initial three units of each book which focus on planet Earth, water and weather. Human geography is considered in units on settlements, work and travel. There is also a unit specifically devoted to the urban and rural environment and human impact on the natural world. This is a very important aspect of modern geography and a key topic for schools generally.

Skills

Maps and plans are introduced in context to convey information about the places which are being studied. The books contain maps at scales which range from the local to global and use a range of techniques which children can emulate. Charts, diagrams and other graphical devices are included throughout. Fieldwork is strongly emphasised and all the books include projects and investigations which can be conducted in the local environment.

Information technology

Geography has always been closely associated with information technology. The way in which computers can be used for recording and processing information is illustrated in each of the books. Satellite images are included together with information from data handling packages. Oblique and vertical aerial photographs are included as sources of evidence.

Cross-curricular links

The different units in *Collins Primary Geography* can be easily linked with other subjects. The physical geography units have natural synergies with themes from sciences, as do the units on the environment. Local area studies overlap with work in history. Furthermore, the opportunities for promoting the core subjects are particularly strong. Each lesson is supported by discussion questions and many of the investigations involve written work in different modes and registers.

Places, themes and skills

Places and Themes	Book 3 Units	Book 4 Units	Book 5 Units	Book 6 Units
Planet Earth	Landscapes	Coasts	Seas and oceans	Restless Earth
Water	Water around us	Rivers	Wearing away the land	Drinking water
Weather	Weather worldwide	Weather patterns	The seasons	Local weather
Settlements	Villages	Towns	Cities	Planning issues
Work and travel	Travel	Food and shops	Jobs	Transport
Environment	Caring for the countryside	Caring for towns	Pollution	Conservation
United Kingdom	Scotland	Northern Ireland	Wales	England
Europe	France	Germany	Greece	Europe
North and South America	South America *Chile*	North America *The Rocky Mountains*	North America *Jamaica*	South America *The Amazon*
Asia and Africa	Asia *India*	Asia *UAE*	Africa *Kenya*	Asia *Singapore*

Layout of the units

Each book is divided into ten units composed of three lessons. In the opening units pupils are introduced to key themes such as water, weather, settlement and the environment at increasing levels of complexity. The following units focus on places from around the UK, Europe and other continents. The overall aim is to provide a balanced coverage of geography.

Unit title
Identifies the focus of the unit and suggests links and connections to other subjects.

Lesson title
Identifies the theme of the lesson. The supporting copymaster also uses this title which makes it easy to identify.

Enquiry question
Suggests opportunities for open-ended investigations and practical activities.

Key word panel
Highlights key geographical words and terms which will be used during the lesson.

Introductory text
Introduces the topic in a graded text of around 100 words.

Discussion panel
Consists of three questions designed to draw pupils into the topic and to stimulate discussion. The first question often involves simple comprehension, the second question involves reasoning and the third question introduces a human element which helps to relate the topic to the child's own experience.

Graphics
Graphical devices ranging from maps to satellite images amplify the topic.

Data Bank
Provides extra information to engage children and encourage them to find out more for themselves.

Mapwork exercise
Indicates how the lesson can be developed through atlas and mapwork.

Investigation panel
Suggests a practical activity which will help pupils consolidate their understanding.

Summary panel
Indicates the knowledge and understanding covered in the unit.

Copymasters
Each lesson has a supporting copymaster which can be found in pages 30-59 of this book.

Layout of the units

Enquiry question

Lesson title

Unit title

Key word panel

Graphic

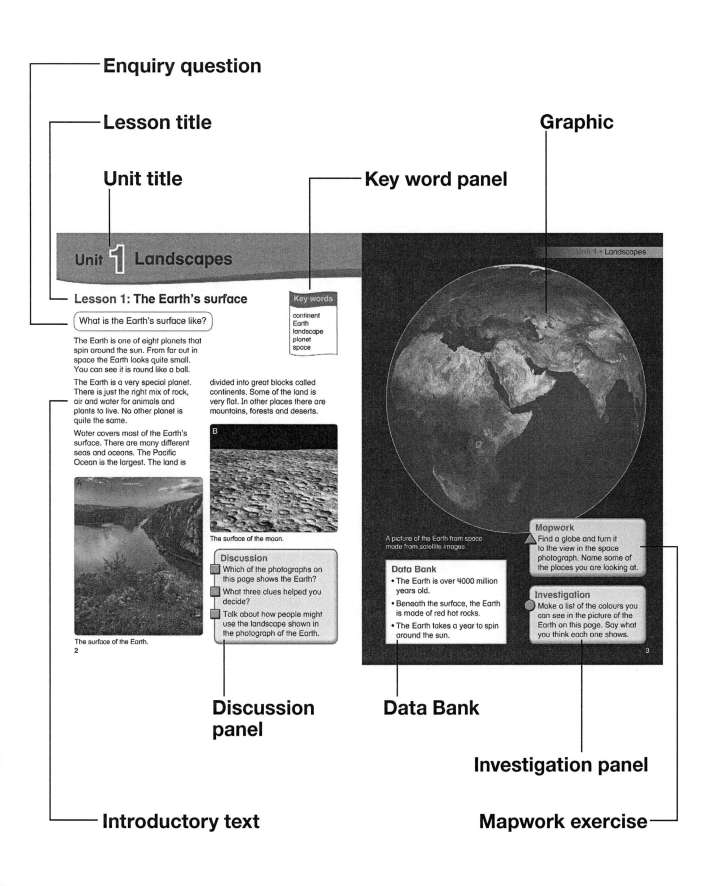

Unit 1 Landscapes

Lesson 1: The Earth's surface

What is the Earth's surface like?

The Earth is one of eight planets that spin around the sun. From far out in space the Earth looks quite small. You can see it is round like a ball.

The Earth is a very special planet. There is just the right mix of rock, air and water for animals and plants to live. No other planet is quite the same.

Water covers most of the Earth's surface. There are many different seas and oceans. The Pacific Ocean is the largest. The land is

divided into great blocks called continents. Some of the land is very flat. In other places there are mountains, forests and deserts.

Key words

continent
Earth
landscape
planet
space

B

The surface of the moon.

A

The surface of the Earth.
2

Discussion
- Which of the photographs on this page shows the Earth?
- What three clues helped you decide?
- Talk about how people might use the landscape shown in the photograph of the Earth.

A picture of the Earth from space made from satellite images.

Data Bank
- The Earth is over 4000 million years old.
- Beneath the surface, the Earth is made of red hot rocks.
- The Earth takes a year to spin around the sun.

Mapwork
Find a globe and turn it to the view in the space photograph. Name some of the places you are looking at.

Investigation
Make a list of the colours you can see in the picture of the Earth on this page. Say what you think each one shows.

3

Discussion panel

Data Bank

Investigation panel

Introductory text

Mapwork exercise

Lesson planning

Collins Primary Geography has been designed to support both whole school and individual lesson planning. As you devise your schemes and work out lesson plans you may find it helpful to ask the following questions. For example, have you:

- Given children a range of entry points which will engage their enthusiasm and capture their imagination?
- Used a range of teaching strategies which cater for pupils who learn in different ways?
- Thought about using games as a teaching device?
- Explored the ways that stories or personal accounts might be integrated with the topic?
- Considered the opportunities for practical activities and fieldwork enquiries?
- Encouraged pupils to use globes and maps where appropriate?
- Considered whether to include a global dimension?
- Checked to see whether you are challenging rather than reinforcing stereotypes?
- Checked on links to suitable websites, particularly with respect to research?
- Made use of ICT to record findings or analyse information?

- Made links to other subjects where there is a natural overlap?
- Promoted geography alongside literacy skills especially in talking and writing?
- Taken advantage of the opportunities for presentations and class displays?
- Ensured that the pupils are developing geographical skills and meaningful subject knowledge?
- Clarified the knowledge, skills and concepts that will underpin the unit?
- Identified appropriate learning outcomes or given pupils the opportunity to identify their own ones?

These questions are offered as prompts which may help you to generate stimulating and lively lessons. There is clear evidence that when geography is fun and pupils enjoy what they are doing it can lead to lasting learning. Striking a balance between light-hearted delivery and serious intent is part of the craft of being a teacher.

Misconceptions

There is a growing body of research which helps practitioners to understand more about how children learn primary geography and the barriers and challenges that they commonly encounter. The way that young children assume that the physical environment was created by people was first highlighted by Jean Piaget. The importance and significance of early childhood misconceptions was further illuminated by Howard Gardner. More recent research has considered how children develop their understanding of maps and places. Children's ideas about other countries and their attitudes to other nationalities form another very important line of enquiry. Some key readings are listed in the references on page 15.

Lesson summary

The table below provides an overview of the lessons in *Collins Primary Geography Pupil Book 3*. Individual schools may want to adapt the lessons and associated activities according to their particular needs and circumstances.

Theme	Unit	Lesson 1	Lesson 2	Lesson 3
Planet Earth	Landscapes	The Earth's surface	The shape of the land	Investigating landscapes
Water	Water around us	A wet planet	The effects of water	Recording water
Weather	Weather worldwide	Different types of weather	Living in hot and cold places	Sunshine matters
Settlements	Villages	A village community	Different types of village	Investigating villages
Work and travel	Travel	Ways of travelling	Finding your way	Routes and journeys
Environment	Caring for the countryside	Wildlife around us	Protecting wildlife	Improving our surroundings
United Kingdom	Scotland	Introducing Scotland	Edinburgh: The capital city of Scotland	Mull: A Scottish Island
Europe	France	Introducing France	Growing food	Making cars
North and South America	South America	Introducing South America	Spotlight on Chile	The Galapagos Islands
Asia and Africa	Asia	Introducing Asia	India: A country in Asia	Pallipadu: A village in India

Studying the local area

The local area is the immediate vicinity around the school and the home. It consists of three different components: the school building, the school grounds, and local streets and buildings. By studying their local area, children will learn about the different features which make their environment distinctive and how it attains a specific character. When they are familiar with their own area, they will then be able to make meaningful comparisons with more distant places.

There are many opportunities to support the lessons outlined in *Collins Primary Geography* with practical local area work. First-hand experience is fundamental to good practice in geography teaching, is a clear requirement in the programme of study and has been highlighted in guidance to Ofsted inspectors. The local area can be used not only to develop ideas from human geography but also to illustrate physical and environmental themes. The checklist below illustrates some of the features which could be identified and studied.

Physical geography	Human geography
Hill, valley, cliff, mountain, rock, slope, soil, wood	Origins of settlements, land use and economic activity
River, stream, pond, lake, estuary, coast	House, cottage, terrace, flat, housing estate
Slopes, rock, soil, plants and other small-scale features	Roads, stations, harbours
Local weather and site conditions	Shops, factories and offices
	Fire, police, ambulance, health services
	Library, museum, park, leisure centre

All work in the local area involves collecting and analysing information. An important way in which this can be achieved is through the use of maps and plans. Other techniques include annotated drawings, bar charts, tables and reports. There will also be opportunities for the children to make presentations in class and perhaps to the rest of the school in assemblies.

Studying places in the UK and wider world

Collins Primary Geography Pupil Book 3 contains studies of the following places in the UK and wider world. Place studies focus on small scale environments and everyday life. By considering people and describing their surroundings, the information is presented at a scale and in a manner which relates particularly well to children. Research shows that pupils tend to reach a peak of friendliness towards other countries and nations at about the age of ten. It is important to capitalise on this educationally and to challenge prejudices and stereotypes.

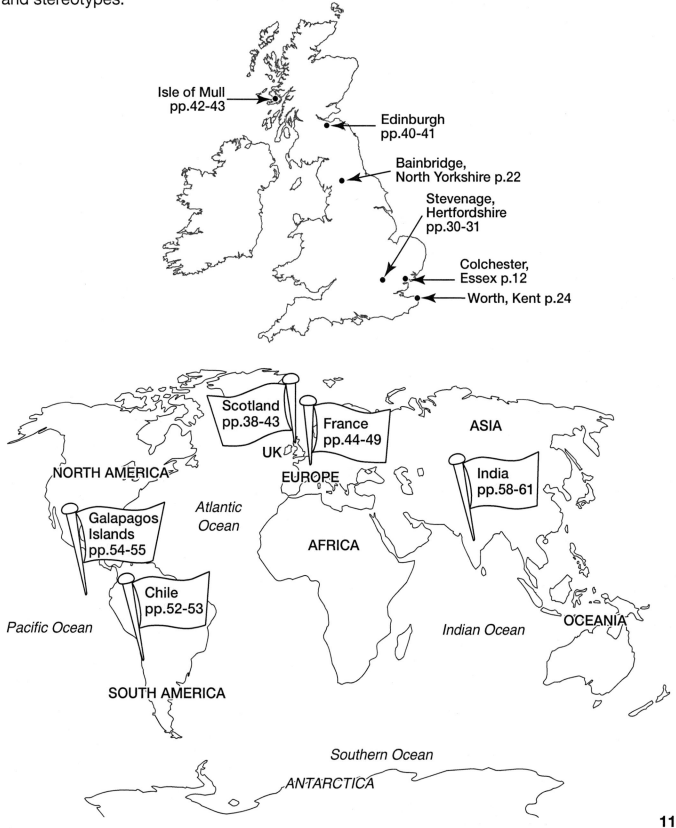

Isle of Mull
pp.42-43

Edinburgh
pp.40-41

Bainbridge,
North Yorkshire p.22

Stevenage,
Hertfordshire
pp.30-31

Colchester,
Essex p.12

Worth, Kent p.24

Scotland
pp.38-43

France
pp.44-49

UK

ASIA

NORTH AMERICA

EUROPE

India
pp.58-61

Atlantic
Ocean

Galapagos
Islands
pp.54-55

AFRICA

Chile
pp.52-53

Pacific Ocean

Indian Ocean

OCEANIA

SOUTH AMERICA

Southern Ocean

ANTARCTICA

Differentiation and progression

Collins Primary Geography sets out to provide access to the curriculum for children of all abilities. It is structured so that children can respond to and use the material in a variety of ways. Within each unit there is a range of exercises and discussion questions. This means activities can be selected which are appropriate to individual circumstances.

Differentiation by outcome

Each lesson starts with an introductory text and linked discussion questions which are designed to capture the children's imagination and draw them into the topic. There are opportunities for slower learners to relate the material to their own experience. More able children will be able to consider the underlying geographical concepts. The pace and range of the discussion can be controlled to suit the needs of the class or group.

Differentiation by process

Children of all abilities benefit from exploring their environment and conducting their own investigations. The investigation activities include many suggestions for direct experience and first-hand learning. Work in the local area can overcome the problems of written communication by focusing on concrete events. There are also opportunities for taking photographs and conducting surveys as well as for making lists, diagrams and written descriptions.

Differentiation by task

The mapwork and investigation exercises can be modified according to the pupils' ability levels. Teachers may decide to complete some of the tasks as class exercises or help slower learners by working through the first part of an exercise with them. Classroom assistants could also use the lessons with individual children or small groups. More able children could be given extension tasks. Ideas and suggestions for extending each lesson are provided in the information on individual units (pages 16-25).

Progression

The themes, language and complexity of the material have been graded to provide progression between each title. However, the gradient between different books is deliberately shallow. This makes it possible for the books to be used interchangeably by different year groups or within mixed ability classes. The way that this might work can be illustrated by considering a sample unit. For instance, in Book 3 the unit on weather introduces children to hot and cold places around the world. Book 4 looks at ways of recording the weather, Book 5 focuses on the seasons and Book 6 considers local weather conditions. This approach provides opportunities for reinforcement and revisiting which will be particularly helpful for the less able child.

Assessment

Assessment is often seen as having two very different dimensions. Formative assessment is an on-going process which provides both pupils and teachers with information about the progress they are making in a piece of work. Summative assessment occurs at defined points in a child's learning and seeks to establish what they have learnt and how they are performing in relation both to their peers and to nationally agreed standards. *Collins Primary Geography* provides opportunities for both formative and summative assessment.

Formative assessment

- The discussion questions invite pupils to discuss a topic, relate it to their previous experience and consider any issues which may arise, thereby yielding information about their current knowledge and understanding.
- The mapwork exercises focus especially on developing spatial awareness and skills and will indicate the pupils' current level of ability
- The investigation activities give pupils the chance to extend their knowledge in ways that match their current abilities.

Summative assessment

- The panels at the end of each unit highlight key learning outcomes. These can be tested directly through individually designed exercises.
- The copymasters (see pages 30-59) can be used to provide additional evidence of pupil achievement. Whether used formatively or summatively they are intended to broaden and consolidate understanding.

Reporting to parents

Collins Primary Geography is structured around geographical skills, themes and place studies which become more complex from one book to another. As children work through the units they can build up a folder of work. This will include mapwork and investigations in the local area and will provide evidence of breadth, progression and achievement in geography. It will also be a useful resource when teachers report to parents about whether an individual child is above average, satisfactory, or in need of help in geography.

National curriculum reporting

There is a single attainment target for geography and other National Curriculum subjects. This simply states that

> *'By the end of each key stage, pupils are expected to know, apply and understand the matters, skills and processes specified in the relevant programme of study.'*

This means that assessment need not be an onerous burden and that evidence of pupils' achievement can be built up over an entire Key Stage. The assessment process can also inform lesson planning. Establishing what pupils have demonstrably understood helps to highlight more clearly what they still need to learn.

High quality geography

The regular reviews of geography teaching in the UK undertaken by Ofsted provide a clear guidance.

Ofsted recommendations

Ofsted recommends schools to:

- focus on developing pupils' core knowledge and sense of place.
- ensure that geography elements are clearly identified within topic based work.
- maximize opportunities for fieldwork in order to improve pupil motivation.
- make the most of new technology to enthuse pupils and provide immediacy and relevance.
- provide more opportunities for writing at length and focused reading.
- enable pupils to recognise their responsibilities as citizens.
- develop networks to share good practice.
- provide subject specific support and professional development opportunities for teachers.

Primary Geography Quality Mark

The Primary Geography Quality Mark set up by the UK Geographical Association is another measure of excellence. This provides a self-assessment framework designed to help subject leaders. There are three categories of award. The 'bronze' level recognises that lively and enjoyable geography is happening in your school, the 'silver' level recognises excellence across the school and the 'gold' level recognises excellence that is shared and embedded in the community beyond the school. The framework is divided into four separate cells (a) pupil progress and achievement (b) quality of teaching (c) behaviour and relationships (d) leadership and management. For further details see www.geography.org.uk.

Achieving accreditation for geography in school is a useful way of badging achievements and identifying targets for future improvement. The Geographical Association provides a wide range of support to help teachers with this process. In addition to an ambassador scheme and Continuing Professional Development (CPD) sessions it produces a journal for primary schools, *Primary Geography*, three time a year. Other key sources are the Geographical Association website, the *Primary Geography Handbook* and books and guides for classroom use such as *Geography Plus*.

Finding time for geography

The pressures on the school timetable and the demands of the core subjects make it hard to secure adequate time for primary geography. However, finding ways of integrating geography with mathematics and literacy can be a creative way of increasing opportunities. Geography also has a natural place in a wide range of social studies and current affairs whether local or global. It can be developed through class assemblies and extra-curricular studies. Those who are committed to thinking geographically find a surprising number of ways of developing the subject whatever the accountability regime in which they operate.

Ofsted inspections

Ofsted inspections are designed to monitor standards of teaching in schools in England and Wales. Curriculum development is an on-going process and inspectors do not always expect to see totally completed programmes. What they are looking for is evidence of carefully planned strategies which are having a positive impact on the quality of teaching. However, inspectors must also note weaknesses and highlight aspects which need attention. If curriculum development is already in hand in your school, it should receive positive support. The following checklist provides prompts which may help prepare for inspections.

1 Identify a teacher who is responsible for developing the geography curriculum.
2 Provide a regular opportunity for discussing geography teaching in staff meetings.
3 See that all members of staff are familiar with the geography curriculum.
4 Decide how geography will fit into your whole school plan.
5 Make an audit of current geography teaching resources to identify gaps and weaknesses.
6 Discuss and develop a geography policy which includes statements on overall aims, topic planning, teaching methods, resources, assessment and recording.
7 Discuss the policy with the governors.
8 Devise an action plan for geography which includes an annual review procedure.

References and further reading

Bonnett, A. (2009) *What is Geography?* London: Sage

Butt, G. (Ed.) (2011) *Geography, Education and the Future,* London: Continuum

Catling, S. and Willy, T. (2009) *Teaching Primary Geography*, Exeter: Learning Matters

DfE (2013) National Curriculum in England: Programmes of study – Key Stages 1 and 2 available at www.education.gov.uk/schools/teachingandlearning/curriculum/primary

Lucas, B. and Claxton, G. (2011) *New Kinds of Smart*, Maidenhead: Open University Press

Martin, F. (2006) *Teaching Geography in Primary Schools : Learning to live in the world*, Cambridge: Kington

Ofsted (2011) *Geography: Learning to Make a World of Difference*, London: Ofsted

Scoffham, S. (Ed.) (2010) *Primary Geography Handbook*, Sheffield: Geographical Association

Scoffham, S. (Ed.) (2013) *Teaching Geography Creatively*, London: Routledge

Wiegand, P. (2006) *Learning and Teaching with Maps*, London: Routledge

The Geographical Association

The Geographical Association (GA) provides extensive support and advice for teachers including a range of excellent publications such as the *Everyday Geography* and *Geography Plus* series. As well as holding an annual conference, the GA also produces a journal for primary practitioners, *Primary Geography*, which is published three times a year. To find out more and learn about the latest developments in geography education visit the website at www.geography.org.uk.

Information on the units

Unit 1: LANDSCAPES

The word 'geography' literally means 'Earth writing'. The way that wind, water, ice and snow have worn away the land is part of the Earth story. The way people have responded to their physical surroundings is the other major strand.

The Earth has a fixed orbit around the sun and has a relatively stable climate. The surface is covered with a mixture of rock, air and water. These unique conditions have enabled life to evolve. The first organisms probably date back 3000 million years. On this timescale human beings are very recent additions as they have only emerged in the last 500,000 years.

Lesson 1: THE EARTH'S SURFACE
What is the Earth's surface like?
Photograph A shows the Earth's surface in the Danube gorge between Serbia and Romania. The most striking features are the water, clouds, blue sky and the flowers and plants in the foreground. Photograph B shows the surface of the moon. It is dry and dusty and there are craters where meteors have crashed to the ground.
Mapwork *Africa, the Middle East and India show up prominently in the foreground. Europe is towards the top of the picture.*
Investigation *Deserts are shown in orange/ yellow, grasslands in light green, forests in deep green and water in blue. You might discuss the difference between images and photographs as an extension.*

Lesson 2: THE SHAPE OF THE LAND
Are all landscapes the same?
The Earth's crust has been shaped over geological time by a complex variety of forces - violent movements, ageing of the rocks, the action of water and erosion. At this stage it is enough for children to be able to identify different types of landscape and to interpret the photographs.
Mapwork *Pupils could create a coloured plasticine model island with labels on a hardboard base, papier mâché models in cardboard boxes are more effective but slower to make.*
Investigation *There will be opportunities for children to continue adding to their notebooks as they complete other lessons.*

Lesson 3: INVESTIGATING LANDSCAPES
What is the landscape like in the British Isles?
This double page spread relates general landscape terms to specific features (a) in the British Isles (b) in the local area. Research indicates that many young children think the landscape has been created by people. You may encounter this misconception as you talk with them about the features of your area.
Mapwork *Children are sometimes confused to discover that the Lake District is a mountain area.*
Investigation *You could develop the investigation by focusing on remarkable landscapes around the world and arrange the pictures around a world map as a class display.*

Copymasters *See 1, 2 and 3 for linked extension exercises.*

Information on the units

Unit 2: WATER AROUND US

Water has a profound influence on our environment. Seas and oceans cover large parts of the Earth's surface. At the poles there are massive sheets of ice which never melt. Most of the water in the world is either salty or frozen. This only leaves a very small portion of fresh water.

People depend on fresh water for their survival. It is essential for drinking, cooking and washing. Modern industry and agriculture also require large quantities of water in order to operate. In some places, water is used to generate hydro-electric power. Elsewhere it is used for irrigation. Where rivers are deep enough they are used by ships and boats. Of all the varied resources on the Earth's surface, water is arguably one of the most important.

Lesson 1: A WET PLANET
Where do we find water?

This double page spread introduces children to one aspect of the water cycle – the processes involved as water droplets fall back to Earth and end up in the sea. You will need to discuss the relationship between ice, water and steam if they are to really understand what happens. It can be particularly hard for young children to appreciate that water vapour is an invisible gas. The idea that glaciers are constantly moving is also problematic.

Mapwork *As they complete this exercise, pupils might look for lakes that are grouped together or for those that form inland drainage areas and which have no link to the sea.*

Investigation *This activity makes links to pupils' home environment and would be best completed as a homework exercise.*

Lesson 2: THE EFFECTS OF WATER
Why is water important?

All forms of life depend on water for survival. The children could consider what other plants and creatures might be included in the picture. Water pollution could be introduced to provide a link to wider environmental issues.

Mapwork *This mapping exercise might be completed by groups using large sheets of paper and marker pens.*

Investigation *You might be able to support the investigation with a fieldwork visit to a pond in or near your school to see at first-hand how it creates a special habitat.*

Lesson 3: RECORDING WATER
How is water shown on maps?

Maps show permanent water features but children will have powerful and immediate experiences of the more temporary effects of water in and around their school grounds. There are opportunities to take photographs of what happens when it rains in your area, using the picture on page 13 as the framework for a wall display.

Mapwork *You could extend the work on simple co-ordinates using maps of your own locality or wider region.*

Investigation *From an early age children will have noticed water running down window panes and across roads and slopes. The investigation builds on this experience and leads children to recognise part of the water cycle sequence.*

Copymasters *See 4, 5 and 6 for linked extension exercises.*

Unit 3: WEATHER WORLDWIDE

There are great variations in weather around the world. The hottest places are in deserts like the Sahara where clear skies allow fierce overhead sunlight to reach the surface. At the Equator the air pressure is generally lower giving rise to the heavy rainfall and humid weather which supports the rainforests. At the Poles the sun is always low in the sky and temperatures are generally very low. The interior of Antarctica is exceptionally cold, partly because it is high above sea level and partly because it lacks the moderating influence of the sea.

Lesson 1: DIFFERENT TYPES OF WEATHER

Is the weather the same all over the world?

The main aim of this double page spread is establish the idea that there are variations of climate around the world and the impact this has on plants and animals. The photographs show the Amazon rainforest, Sahara Desert and Antarctica.

Mapwork *When the children add the new terms to their notebooks encourage them to include maps.*

Investigation *The children might make origami paper fortune tellers with questions about weather records linked to each of the quadrants.*

Lesson 2: LIVING IN HOT AND COLD PLACES

How do people live in hot and cold places?

Plants and animals have been able to adapt to different climates over long periods of time. People, on the other hand, use technology to help them survive in challenging conditions. This contrast is something which the children should discuss as they find out about living in Greenland and a hot desert oasis.

Mapwork *Use aerial photographs and images from Google Earth to help children make their picture maps and models.*

Investigation *Pupils might consider different categories when they complete this exercise e.g. clothing, food, houses, transport, plants and animals.*

Lesson 3: SUNSHINE MATTERS

Why are some places hot and other places cold?

The world map shows the distribution of rainforest, desert and polar climates. In order to understand it children need to appreciate that the overhead sun is extremely powerful and that the more the sun's rays slant the weaker they become. This is explained in the diagram above the map.

Mapwork *Extend the mapwork by getting children to name other polar, desert and rainforest areas.*

Investigation *The idea that some parts of the school grounds resemble desert or rainforest regions brings the ideas in this unit back to the child's personal experience.*

Copymasters *See 7, 8 and 9 for linked extension exercises.*

Unit 4: VILLAGES

Nearly all the villages in Britain today were founded before the Norman conquest in 1066. The sites that were chosen reflect a variety of different needs such as food, shelter, communication and defence. In some country areas, fresh water came to the surface in springs along a particular contour line giving rise to a row of villages. Around the coast, fishing villages were built to take advantage of natural features such as bays and headlands. Nowadays many of the people who live in villages have jobs in nearby towns and cities. Others have decided to retire to the countryside. The result is that there have been irreversible changes in rural life.

Lesson 1: A VILLAGE COMMUNITY
What makes a village?

This double page spread focuses on a Martian community in order to show how a village meets a range of different needs. It illustrates how people benefit from collaboration and mutual support. It also highlights the ecological and environmental basis on which we all depend.

Mapwork *Identfying how different parts of a school cater for our needs illustrates the idea of a community at an immediate scale which children can comprehend.*

Investigation *The investigation might be completed as a homework activity with information recorded on a simple outline plan.*

Lesson 2: DIFFERENT TYPES OF VILLAGE
Are all villages the same?

The study of Bainbridge in North Yorkshire shows how people have made use of their physical surroundings (the Pennines) in a real life situation. The photographs on the opposite page (page 23) introduce a global dimension and highlight how traditional housing responds to variations in climate and natural resources.

Mapwork *This is a good opportunity to introduce pupils to an Ordnance Survey map of their area in a quest which many will find both stimulating and enjoyable.*

Investigation *Drawing pictures from the photographs will encourage children to engage with the details of the images and gets them to think about the differences.*

Lesson 3: INVESTIGATING VILLAGES
How do villages change?

Worth is an ancient village in Kent which grew up around a church and village green. In Victorian times it spread westwards towards the main road as the population of the area increased. Change is a constant feature in all settlements and Worth can be expected to evolve in the future just as it has developed in the past.

Mapwork *You might extend the activity by getting children to look at a large scale plan of the school locality where they should be able to find plans of the houses where they live.*

Investigation *If your school is in a built up area you could focus on a single nearby street. Remember that children find it hard to distinguish between old and new buildings and are often misled by superficial clues such as peeling paintwork or imitation lead windows. If you can find old maps and documents, these will help to support fieldwork observations.*

Copymasters *See 10, 11 and 12 for linked extension activities.*

Unit 5: TRAVEL

One of the features of the modem world is that people are travelling further and at greater speeds than ever before. In the 1930s, for example, it used to take 16 days to travel from Britain to Barbados by sea. The same journey can now be done in eight hours by air.

Good communications are essential to modem economic activity. Grain and foodstuffs are grown in one country and transported to another. Oil from the Middle East provides power for industries thousands of kilometres away. Meanwhile, tropical islands have become popular holiday destinations for Europeans. Such links and connections, multiplied thousands of times, are the hallmarks of globalisation.

Lesson 1: WAYS OF TRAVELLING
What different types of transport are there?
The collage of photographs and drawings on pages 26 and 27 brings together the diverse perceptions that children have of transport. Although the technology has changed over the past 150 years, the issues remain basically the same. Questions around the terrain, cargo, distance, speed and environmental impact combine to influence the decisions people make.
Mapwork *Children could extend the timeline into the future to explore their ideas about what might happen next.*
Investigation *The children could represent their findings in a chart or diagram thus making links with mathematics.*

Lesson 2: FINDING YOUR WAY
Why do people use maps?
Formal maps – maps which follow agreed rules – enable us to communicate spatial information to other people. Informal maps – the maps we carry in our heads – provide additional and very useful information. In real life most of us use a mixture of informal and formal maps as we navigate from place to place.
Mapwork *The children could show alternative routes which would be of interest to different types of visitor.*
Investigation *Maps appear in all sorts of places such as tea towels, mugs, postcards, brochures and tickets. Encourage the children to contribute a range of different examples as you build up the display.*

Lesson 3: ROUTES AND JOURNEYS
Do routes matter?
The journey from Burydale School to the swimming pool illustrates how we use landmarks to help us navigate. It also introduces the idea of alternative routes and diversions.
Mapwork *Ask the children to look for the landmarks they pass on their journey to school before they draw their route map.*
Investigation *You might consider the environmental impact of different forms of transport and the advantages of walking when children complete this investigation.*

Copymasters *See 13, 14 and 15 for linked extension exercises.*

Unit 6: CARING FOR THE COUNTRYSIDE

There has been an enormous expansion of industry and population around the world over the last century. The discovery of nuclear fission, the use of electricity and other technological innovations have brought immense changes. For the first time in history people now have the ability to influence the balance of life on Earth. This new power has brought with it the realisation that the Earth is a fragile planet. Either we live in harmony with our surroundings or we risk destroying our ecological base. This unit lays the foundations for exploring environmental issues by focusing on habitats and wildlife conservation.

Lesson 1: WILDLIFE AROUND US
What is a habitat?

The picture shows how a piece of undisturbed wasteland can be a valuable habitat. In order to decide where each animal would live, the children will have to discuss their needs. Some animals live in damp, shady places for protection; others prefer dry, sunny places. The children may be able to find several suitable sites in the picture

Mapwork *This activity relates the notion of habitats to the pupils' own environment.*

Investigation *Some children are likely to live in houses where the front gardens have been paved to create parking spaces. In these circumstances it will be more constructive to talk about how such environments can still be made more friendly to plants and creatures rather than criticising what has happened.*

Lesson 2: PROTECTING WILDLIFE
What are people doing to care for plants and animals?

This double page spread takes a global perspective and identifies problems from around the world. The photographs illustrate how people are trying to solve environmental problems. Taking a positive angle is important in empowering children so they do not turn off in the face of difficulties.

Mapwork *This is a good opportunity to use picture maps to create engaging and inviting images.*

Investigation *Encourage the children to use maps, diagrams and geographical data in their posters so they stay focused geographically.*

Lesson 3: IMPROVING OUR SURROUNDINGS
What happens at a nature reserve?

This lesson illustrates how people are caring for the environment in built up and semi-rural areas. Blean Woods nature reserve is on the edge of Canterbury in Kent. Byron School is in the middle of a town. Even here there are many opportunities for small scale improvement projects. It is also worth remembering that such activities may sow the seeds for a lasting interest in nature and the environment.

Mapwork *You might get the children to present their maps and new designs to the rest of the class as part of their work in Literacy.*

Investigation *You might contact local wildlife groups to see if they can visit your class to talk about their work before the children start to make their nature trails.*

Copymasters *See 16, 17 and 18 for linked extension activities*

Unit 7: UNITED KINGDOM

This unit focuses on Scotland, the most northerly country in the United Kingdom. Scotland has a third of the total land area of the UK but at 5.3 million the population is considerably less than a tenth. Within Scotland there are marked regional variations. The uplands have great empty areas: most activity is concentrated in the central lowlands.

Since the 1970s Scotland has developed as the centre for the North Sea oil industry. This has helped to replace traditional heavy industries such as iron, steel, coal mining and ship building. Ski resorts and conifer plantations are important new developments in the countryside. There has also been growing support for Scottish nationalism.

Lesson 1: INTRODUCING SCOTLAND
What is Scotland like?

This double page spread provides a general introduction to Scotland with information on both physical and human geography. If your school is in Scotland you might use this spread to help you to deliver some of the specific requirements of the Environmental Studies curriculum. If your school is outside Scotland, the map, photographs and text will serve to expand the children's understanding about this part of the United Kingdom.

Mapwork *This activity will get children to look closely at maps of Scotland and introduces them to its unique physical features.*

Investigation *You might supplement the investigations suggested on page 39 by finding out about fishing, agriculture and other industries as part of a wider project on Scotland.*

Lesson 2: EDINBURGH: THE CAPITAL CITY OF SCOTLAND

The introduction provides a simple explanation of why Edinburgh occupies its present site. The growth of settlements involves both a historical and geographical dimension. This is explored in greater detail in subsequent books.

Mapwork *The landmarks shown on the map highlight some of the features which give Edinburgh its character. Le Puy in central France is another city which , like Edinburgh, is set in an old volcanic landscape.*

Investigation *Pupils might imagine that they are selecting places for children of their own age, family groups or overseas visitors as they investigate different sites.*

Lesson 3: MULL: A SCOTTISH ISLAND

Some children will have been to an island on their holidays and will be able to identify with Roy and Christine. However you should also make sure that the rest of the class know what an island is. The fact that Roy and Christine have to travel by ferry and that the map shows Mull surrounded by water are important clues.

Mapwork *Encourage the children to enhance their maps by adding symbols, keys and a north point and outlining the coast of the islands in blue.*

Investigation *The west coast of Scotland provides a distinctive and valuable habitat for plants and animals. You could develop this activity as part of a project on the environment.*

Copymasters *See 19, 20 and 21 for linked extension activities.*

Information on the units

Unit 8: FRANCE

France is the second largest country in Europe after the Ukraine with a population of 64 million people. About one-fifth of the population lives in the largest city Paris. France is in the forefront of modern technology. A network of high-speed railway lines links Paris with other European capitals. Over half of the country's electricity comes from nuclear energy and many new hi-tech industries have been set up, particularly around Grenoble and Toulouse. However France also has a strong agricultural base. It is a major producer of wheat, beef and dairy products and it has one of the largest wine industries in the world.

Lesson 1: INTRODUCING FRANCE
What is France like?

The map of France on page 44 shows physical features and major cities. It is valuable to discuss the shape of the country, the location of the cities and the position of France in relation to the UK. Parnac and Flins are marked because they are studied in the rest of the unit.

Mapwork *There are a considerable number of ferry routes so you might get pupils to concentrate on those that are most popular or well known.*

Investigation *When thinking about links with France, remember to consider physical geography (geology, climate, vegetation) as well as cultural and economic factors.*

Lesson 2: GROWING FOOD
What crops do French farmers grow?

Pamac (Lot) is a small village to the west of Cahors. This lowland area is suitable for a wide range of crops. As you discuss the photograph, remember to talk about how the physical setting influences agriculture.

Mapwork *The mapwork activity introduces notions of distance and scale which you might want to develop further using local or UK maps.*

Investigation *Most of the crops grown in Parnac can also be produced in the UK but they grow better in the warmer climate.*

Lesson 3: MAKING CARS
Where do Renault cars come from?

Renault has a number of factories in different parts of France. It also has factories in other European countries (Spain, Portugal, Belgium and Slovenia). This means that an individual factory, such as the one at Flins, is part of a much wider network.

Mapwork *To complete the mapwork exercise pupils need to scrutinise the map on page 48.*

Investigation *You could extend the survey by asking children to record 50 vehicles and to show the countries where they were made on a map.*

Copymasters *See 22, 23 and 24 for linked extension exercises.*

Information on the units

Unit 9: SOUTH AMERICA

Many people in the UK associate South America with the Amazon rainforest which extends approximately ten degrees north and south of the Equator. Other landscapes include the grasslands of the pampas, the deserts of Patagonia and the high plateaux of the Andes. Big cities are also a significant feature of South America. Rapid urban development has led to four-fifths of the population living in built up areas.

Lesson 1: INTRODUCING SOUTH AMERICA
What is South America like?

Surprisingly few children in UK schools have family links with South America so this introductory lesson will be important in developing their knowledge of the continent. Football and sporting links may provide a natural starting point for discussion. Finding out about volcanoes would provide an entirely different dimension.

Mapwork *The mapwork activity highlights how most parts of South America are in the southern hemisphere.*

Investigation *Pupils could focus on (a) physical (b) human or (c) a mixture of features when they select their points of interest.*

Lesson 2: SPOTLIGHT ON CHILE
What is Chile like?

Chile is a particularly interesting country to choose as a case study for primary school children. The unusual shape and contrasting environments can capture their imagination. The Spanish influence provides a link with history. The country is both remote from their experience but culturally surprisingly familiar.

Mapwork *This exercise directs children's attention towards the outline shape of countries. An extension would be to look for countries which are (a) generally square in shape (b) divided into islands.*

Investigation *Pupils could develop their quizzes by adding questions about other South American countries.*

Lesson 3: THE GALAPAGOS ISLANDS
What is special about the Galapagos Islands?

There are 18 main islands in the Galapagos and many smaller ones. It was the difference in natural life between the islands (especially tortoises and finches) which led Charles Darwin to develop the theory of evolution in the nineteenth century. The scope to link this lesson with work in science is immediately apparent.

Mapwork *You might extend this exercise by asking children to select an island of their choice for a class display on the Galapagos.*

Investigation *The zigzag books will give pupils a framework to structure individual or group research.*

Copymasters *See 25, 26 and 27 for linked extension exercises.*

Information on the units

Unit 10: ASIA

Three-fifths of the people in the world live in Asia. There are nearly 1400 million Chinese, and India has a population of around 1250 million. However Asia is such a vast continent that large areas are almost completely uninhabited, particularly in the mountains of China and Tibet, and the plains of Siberia. In some regions there are huge pressures on the environment. For example, China suffers serious air pollution and toxic waste has made significant areas of Russia uninhabitable.

Lesson 1: INTRODUCING ASIA
What is Asia like?

Children are sometimes puzzled to learn that although Asia is a continent it is actually joined to Europe. The reason for this is historical. The Ancient Greeks were unaware of the lands to the east of the Caspian Sea and believed that Europe was surrounded by water. Nowadays the Ural Mountains are regarded as the boundary between the two continents although some geographers also think of Eurasia as a single entity.

Mapwork *Making a list of Asian countries will encourage children to interrogate an atlas map of the region and may lead them to ask questions to explore and investigate further.*

Investigation *The photographs show four landscape types but pupils could do their own research to discover other examples – the tundra in northern Siberia would be an obvious addition.*

Lesson 2: INDIA: A COUNTRY IN ASIA
What is India like?

In many ways India reflects the scale and diversity of Asia itself. You might want to consider devising a substantial geography focused topic on India. There is certainly plenty of scope to supplement the basic introduction provided in this lesson, particularly if children in your school or community have direct links with the Asian sub-continent.

Mapwork *Children will need to work from an atlas to list the countries around India. They might include Sri Lanka which is a close neighbour.*

Investigation *The zigzag books could be of varying sizes and formats and will make an attractive classroom display.*

Lesson 3: PALLIPADU: A VILLAGE IN INDIA
What is life like in an Indian village?

Although India has many modern cities and hi-tech industries, the villages are still the heartland of the nation. The case study of Pallipadu provides information about physical and human geography and the changes that are taking place in a typical south Indian context. Remember that pupils may approach this study with negative images of India gleaned from peers and the media so stressing positive aspects will provide a counter-balance.

Mapwork *The key buildings marked on the map will help children gain a deeper understanding of what makes the village distinctive.*

Investigation *Setting up a link with an Indian school is a natural way to extend and deepen the investigation.*

Copymasters *See 28, 29 and 30 for linked extension exercises.*

Copymaster matrix

Unit	Copymaster	Description
Landscape	1 The Earth's surface	Pupils colour and compare the pictures of the Earth and the moon.
	2 The shape of the land	The children make drawings of four different landscapes and link them to a diagram.
	3 Investigating landscapes	Pupils complete four pictures to show activities in a landscape context.
Water	4 A wet planet	The children make drawings of an iceberg, snow, sea, rain and a lake.
	5 The effects of water	Children add drawings of creatures to replicate the picture in the book.
	6 Recording water	Pupils cut out labelled pictures to create a flow diagram.
Weather	7 Different types of weather	The children colour and colour and compare pictures of the desert, rainforest and polar lands.
	8 Living in hot and cold places	The children annotate a drawing of a scene from polar lands.
	9 Sunshine matters	Pupils complete the diagram of the sun's rays and compare continents.
Settlement	10 A village community	Pupils identify the purpose of the external and internal features of a house.
	11 Different types of village	Working from a plan the children identify different features of a West African village.
	12 Investigating villages	The children make their own plan of a village by arranging pictures of buildings and other features.
Work and travel	13 Ways of travelling	An introductory activity in which children relate vehicles and journeys.
	14 Finding your way	Pupils analyse three different journeys then add some examples of their own.
	15 Routes and journeys	Working from a picture map, the children identify landmarks along two different routes.

Aim	Teaching point
To show how water is crucial to life.	You might talk about the possibility of life on other planets and what it would require.
To reinforce recognition of important landscape features.	The children could make up their own pictures or work from the pupil book.
To illustrate the connection between physical and human geography.	You could extend this activity by making a display of how people use the landscape.
To show that water can be a liquid, solid or gas.	None of the photographs show water as a gas because water vapour is invisible.
To get children to interrogate the information in the pupil book.	Discuss how a pond has or could enhance your school environment.
To show what happens to water when it reaches the ground.	You will need to provide the children with scissors, glue and strips of paper.
To compare weather and vegetation in different climate zones.	Discuss other climate zones around the world such as alpine, temperate and sub-arctic.
To help children identify features in a photograph and the skills involved in annotation.	Ask the children to make an annotated drawing of the Moroccan oasis by way of extension.
To establish the importance of the sun and its height in the sky.	This exercise compares the Equator and the North Pole so Antarctica is not included on the continents' map.
To illustrate how our need for shelter, warmth and protection is reflected in house design.	Some of the features identified in the labels perform overlapping functions so might be counted twice.
To help children relate a photograph and a plan of the same place.	Be careful not to reinforce stereotypes – many West Africans live in modern blocks of flats.
To consolidate children's understanding of a village through a practical mapwork exercise.	It is important that the children draw the roads and other features such as streams before they glue down the buildings.
To show why different forms of transport are needed.	Read the children a story about a journey as an extension activity.
To show that people make journeys for a variety of reasons.	You could use the information which the children have collected about their own journeys to make a bar chart.
To help children to recognise that landmarks help us to navigate.	Look at aerial photographs of your own locality as an extension activity and compare different ways of reaching the same destination.

Copymaster matrix

Unit	Copymaster	Description
Environment	16 Wildlife around us	The children decide where different creatures might be living in the school grounds and then check to see if they were correct.
	17 Protecting wildlife	Pupils colour pictures of different conservation projects around the world.
	18 Improving our surroundings	Working from a site plan, pupils decide what creatures they might see on school trail.
United Kingdom	19 Introducing Scotland	Children complete an outline map of Scotland with chief cities and relief features.
	20 Edinburgh	Pupils cut out three picture strips to create a silhouette of the Edinburgh skyline.
	21 Mull: A Scottish island	The children link pictures and labels to an outline map of Mull.
Europe	22 Introducing France	Children colour an outline map of France, name some key features and identify surrounding countries.
	23 Growing food	Pupils complete a survey about the physical and human aspects of a French village.
	24 Making cars	Working from a plan pupils identity different areas of a car factory and some of the jobs people do.
North and South America	25 Introducing South America	Using landscape symbols pupils identify different regions in South America together with some key cities.
	26 Spotlight on Chile	Pupils label six artefacts and say how they provide information about Chile.
	27 The Galapagos Islands	Pupils link drawings of creatures to a map of the Galapagos.
Asia and Africa	28 Introducing Asia	Pupils add information to a blank outline map of Asia.
	29 India: A country in Asia	Children create a portrait of India by completing four different information panels.
	30 Pallipadu: A village in India	Children relate the drawings of landmarks to a street plan of Pallipadu.

Aim	Teaching point
To introduce the notion of habitats in a familiar setting and to promote activity learning.	There are good opportunities for linking this work with studies in science.
To indicate that there is a variety of ways people are trying to safeguard biodiversity.	There is an opportunity to extend this study by finding out more about the work of conservation groups such as Greenpeace and WWF.
To provide a model for a simple trail which pupils could adapt and modify in their own locality.	Making a trail is surprisingly time consuming, but like all fieldwork is liable to lead to deep learning.
To help children gain familiarity with key human and physical geography features.	Given the complexity of the outline it may be best for children to show the sea with a thin blue line around the coast.
To introduce children to some key Edinburgh landmarks through a practical activity.	You could adapt this idea to make a skyline silhouette of your own locality.
To develop landscape vocabulary in a meaningful context.	Check that the children understand the meaning of the symbols on the map.
To help children identify the distinctive shape of France and its location in Western Europe.	Pupils could add additional features to the map either individually or in groups.
To explore the range of features which gives a place its character.	The survey questions could be applied to other locations if you want to make other comparisons.
To show that many different people and activities are involved in making a car.	The children might think of other jobs which are done at the factory and the areas involved.
To introduce children to the map of South America.	Pupils could add and name individual rivers, mountains, seas and islands to make their maps more detailed.
To illustrate how artefacts can be used as evidence about a country or environment.	You could develop this activity by setting up a display of artefacts from Chile or South America.
To illustrate how islands in the Galapagos have distinctive wildlife.	Find about more about the life of Charles Darwin and his theory of evolution as an extension activity.
To explore the physical environment and other features of Asia.	Discuss and identify the other continents shown on the map and their boundaries.
To help children find out more about India using different methods of presentation.	Develop the portrait of India by adding information panels about people (e.g. Gandhi), history, animals and so forth.
To explore the distinctive character of an Indian village.	Pupils could add other features to the map working from the plan on page 60.

1 The Earth's surface

Name ....

1. Colour the pictures of the Earth and the moon.

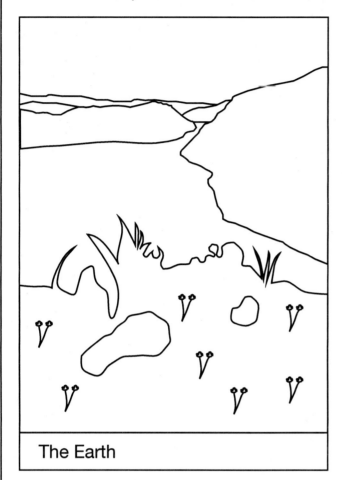

The Earth

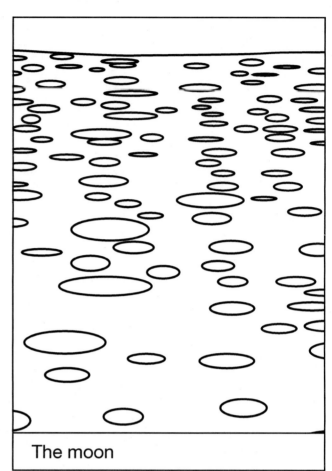

The moon

2. Tick the features which are found on the Earth and the moon.

Earth		Moon	
Air	☐	Air	☐
Water	☐	Water	☐
Soil	☐	Soil	☐
Plants	☐	Plants	☐
Food	☐	Food	☐

3. Complete this sentence.

The two most important things for life on Earth are _____

and _____ .

2 The shape of the land

Name ....

1. Draw a line from each box to the right place on the diagram.

2. Draw a landscape picture in each box.

3. Colour in the pictures you have drawn.

mountains	coast

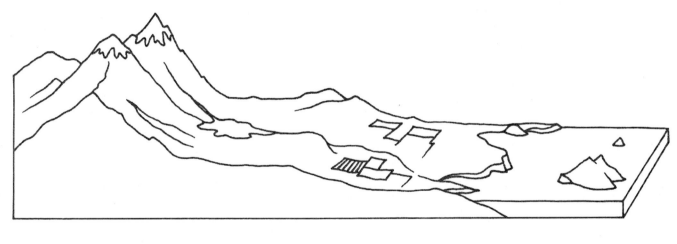

hills and valleys	island

1. Draw a landscape around each of these pictures.

2. Write the words where they belong.

mountain   hills and valley   lowland   coast

4 A wet planet

Name ....

1. Draw a picture to match the word at the top of each box.

2. Is the water in each picture a solid, a liquid or a gas?

Tick the right box.

Iceberg
liquid ☐   solid ☐   gas ☐

Snow
liquid ☐   solid ☐   gas ☐

Sea
liquid ☐   solid ☐   gas ☐

Rain
liquid ☐   solid ☐   gas ☐

Lake
liquid ☐   solid ☐   gas ☐

1. Draw the missing plants and animals in the circles.

2. Complete the sentences.

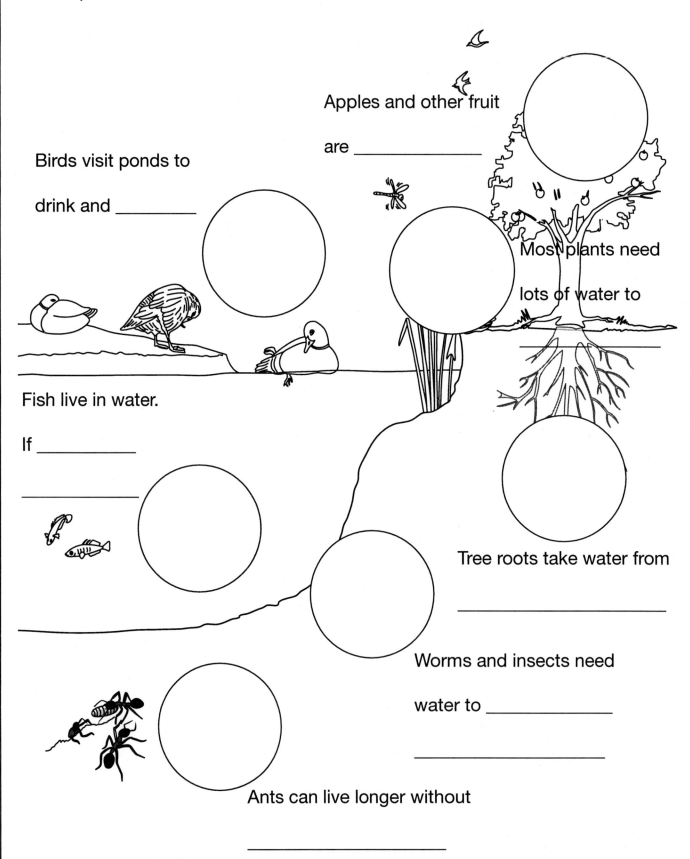

Apples and other fruit

are _____

Birds visit ponds to

drink and _____

Most plants need

lots of water to

_____

Fish live in water.

If _____

_____

Tree roots take water from

_____

Worms and insects need

water to _____

_____

Ants can live longer without

_____

6 Recording water

Name ....

1. Read the sentences and colour the pictures.

2. Cut them out.

3. Glue the pictures in the right order on a strip of paper.

4. Draw arrows to join the pictures together.

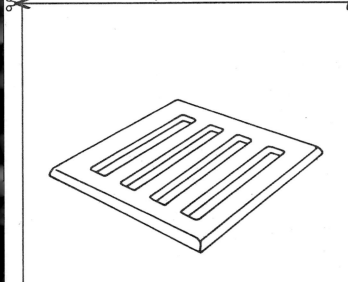

The water goes into the drain.

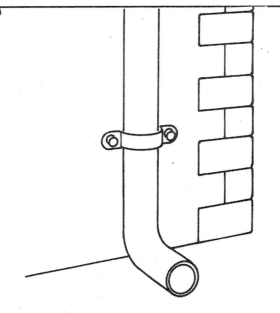

It flows down the drainpipe.

Rain falls from the cloud.

It runs off the roof into the gutter.

1. Colour the pictures.

2. What colours did you use? Finish these sentences.

I used .... for the desert because...

I used .... for the polar lands because...

I used .... for the rainforest because...

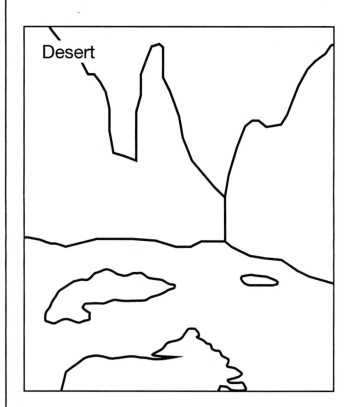

Desert

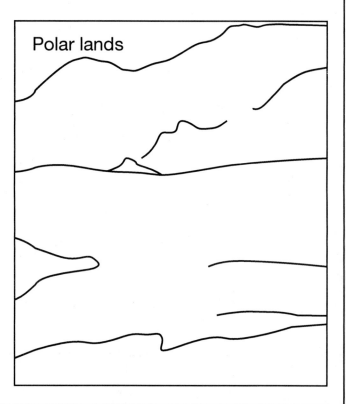

Polar lands

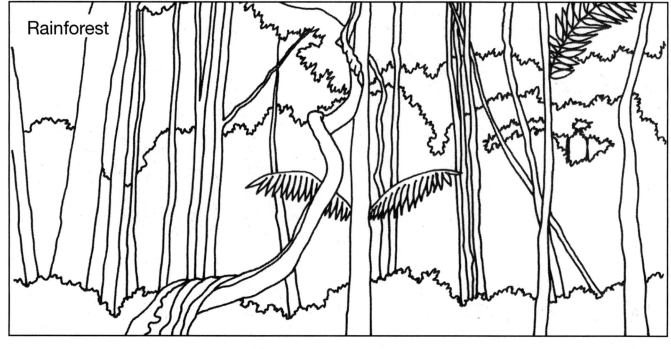

Rainforest

Name ....

1. Write the words in the correct box around the picture.

snowy mountains   bare, rocky slopes

floating ice   thick clothes   fishing boats

2. What things are the same in the United Kingdom? What things are different?

Write a few sentences on a piece of paper.

Primary Geography Pupil Book 3: Weather worldwide pp16-17

1. Fill in the missing labels on the diagram of the Earth.

2. Draw pictures to show why it is cold at the North Pole and not at the Equator.

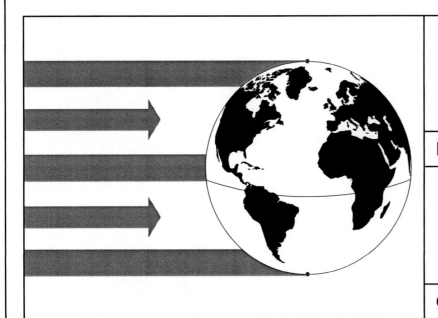

Low sun at North Pole

Overhead sun at the Equator

3. Colour the map. Use green for continents which are near to the North Pole. Use yellow for continents which are near the Equator.

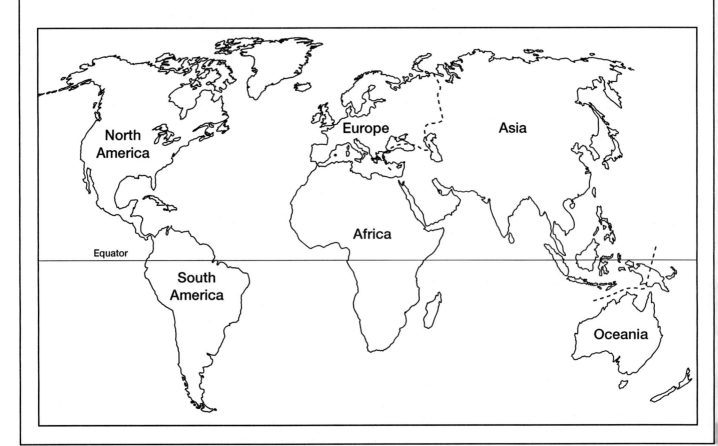

Name ....

1. Copy the labels into the correct boxes to show what each thing does outside a house.

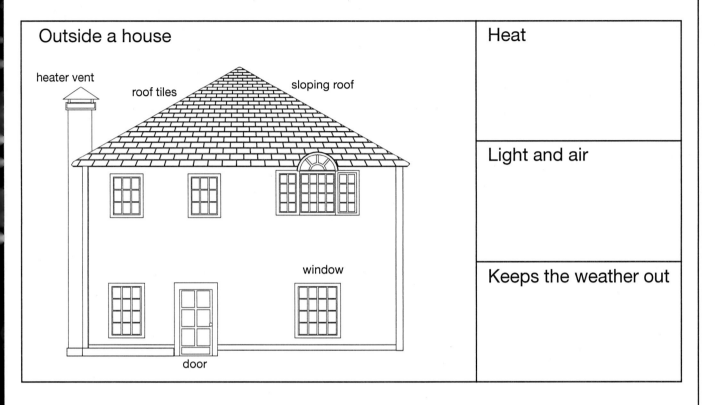

Outside a house	Heat
	Light and air
	Keeps the weather out

2. Copy the labels into the correct boxes to show what each thing does inside a house.

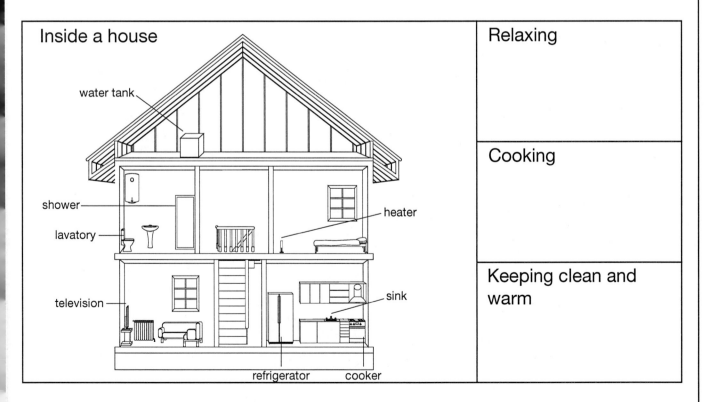

Inside a house	Relaxing
	Cooking
	Keeping clean and warm

11 Different types of villages

Name ....

1. Colour the boxes in the key.

2. Colour the plan of the village in Burkina Faso using the colours in the key.

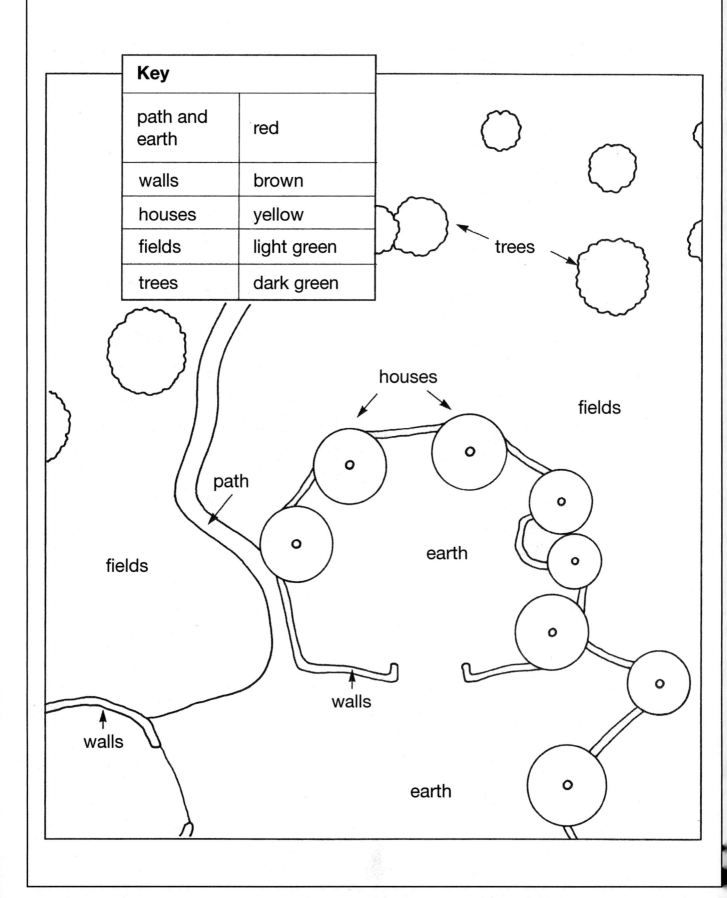

Key

path and earth	red
walls	brown
houses	yellow
fields	light green
trees	dark green

trees

houses

fields

path

fields

earth

walls

walls

earth

1. Colour the pictures.   2. Cut out the boxes.

3. Arrange the pictures on a piece of paper to make a village with roads and buildings.

4. Glue the pictures down.   5. Add some more drawings.

farmhouse   pond   inn

school   church   shop

bungalow   modern house   terraced houses

1. Draw the right vehicles on the pictures below.

ferry   plane   bus   train

1. Label the drawings. Use these words.

    van driver   walker   train passenger

2. Draw a picture of the thing they travelled along.

3. Write down a reason for each journey.

Person making the journey	What they travelled along (path, road or railway)	Reason for Journey

4. Now answer the questions about a journey you have made.

Where did you go? ....

What did you travel in? ....

What did you travel along? ....

Why did you make the journey? ....

Name ....

1. Ruth goes to school by bus. Draw her route to school on the map.

2. Write down some landmarks she passes.

1	
2	
3	

3. David walks to school. Draw his route on the map.

4. Write down some landmarks he passes.

1	
2	
3	

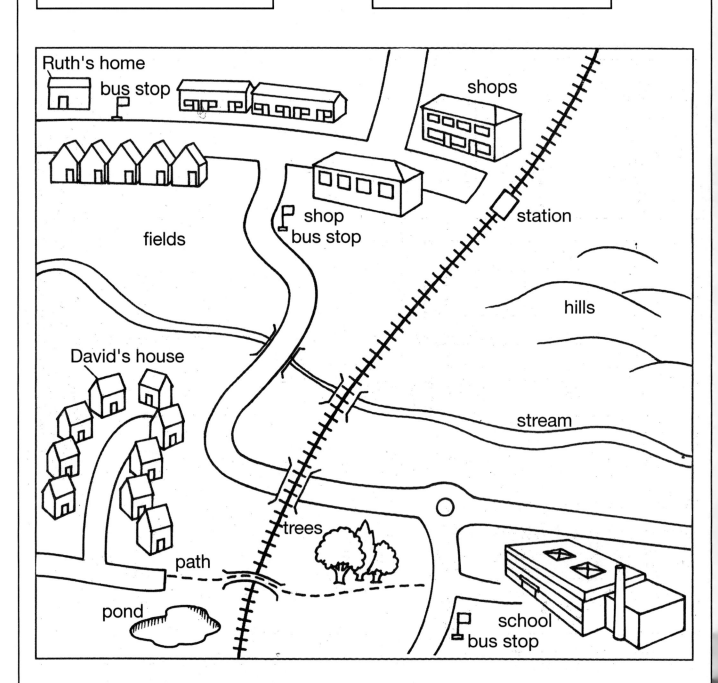

Ruth's home
bus stop
shops
shop
bus stop
fields
station
hills
David's house
stream
trees
path
pond
school
bus stop

Name ....

1. Write the names under the pictures.

    worm   daisy   snail   woodlouse   spider

2. Where might each thing live around your school?

3. Visit the places to find out if you were right.

4. Circle 'yes' or 'no' to show your answer.

Living thing	Places where it might live (habitat)	Can I find it?
		Yes No
		Yes No
		Yes No
		Yes No
		Yes No

17 Protecting wildlife

Name ....

1. Colour the pictures of the conservation projects.

2. Write a sentence about each one.

Improving our surroundings   *Name* ....

1. Write down the animals you might see on this school trail.

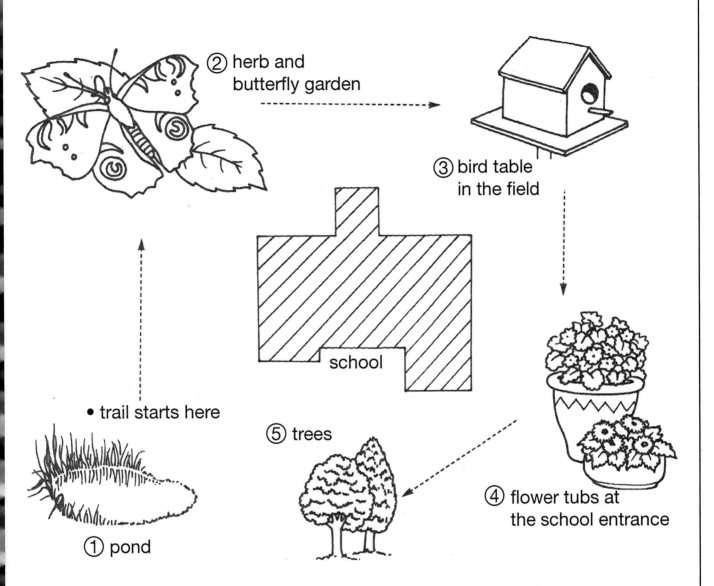

② herb and butterfly garden

③ bird table in the field

• trail starts here

⑤ trees

school

① pond

④ flower tubs at the school entrance

Stop	What animals might you see at this place?
1	
2	
3	
4	
5	

2. Make a list of different habitats in your school.

3. Work out a trail that links these places together.

Name ....

1. Colour the map and key.

   Use green for lowland, brown for highland and blue for sea.

2. Write the names of the cities next to the dots.

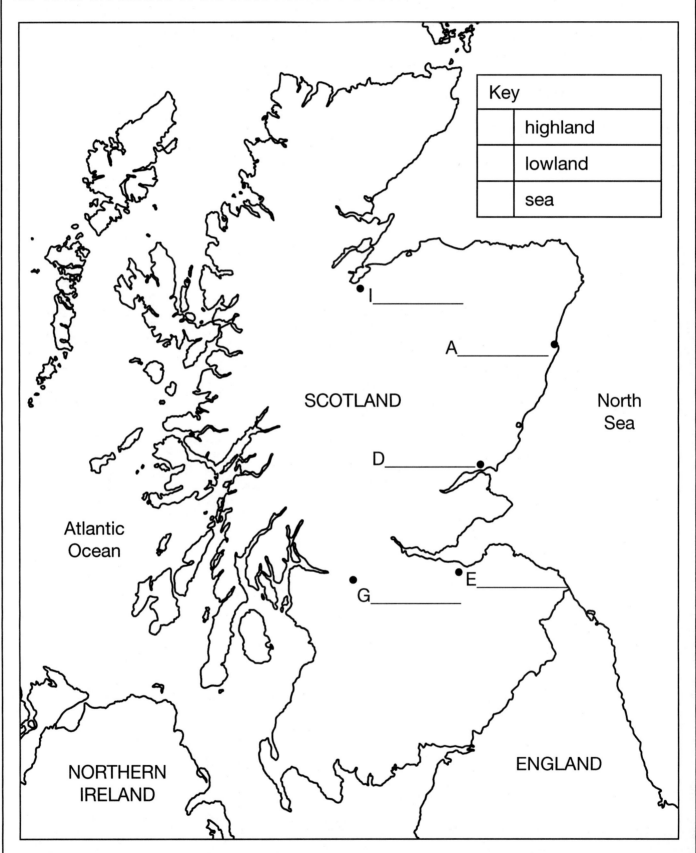

Key

	highland
	lowland
	sea

SCOTLAND

North Sea

Atlantic Ocean

I_____

A_____

D_____

E_____

G_____

NORTHERN IRELAND

ENGLAND

Name ....

1. Cut out the three silhouettes.

2. Join them together in the order they appear on the Edinburgh skyline.

3. Label the landmarks.

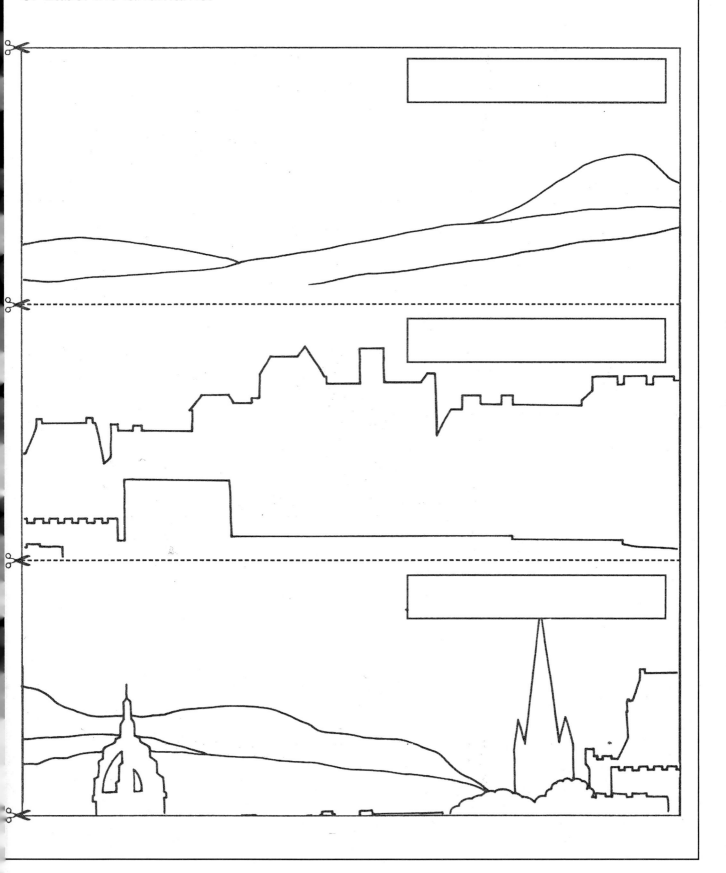

Name ....

1. Draw a line from each picture to its symbol on the map.

2. Draw a line from each symbol to the right label in the box.

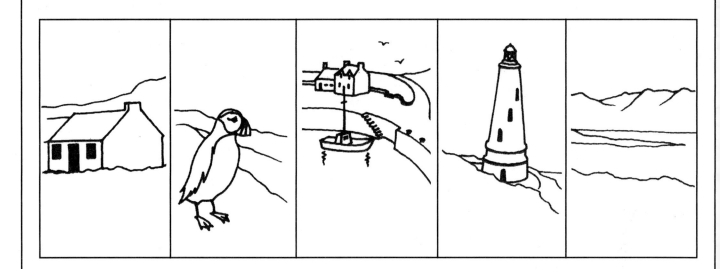

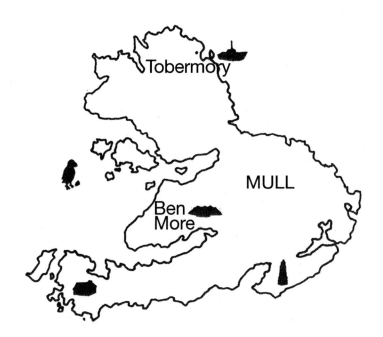

| puffin | mountain | croft | harbour | lighthouse |

22 Introducing France

Name ....

1. Colour the boxes in the key.

2. Shade in the map using these colours.

3. Write in the missing names.

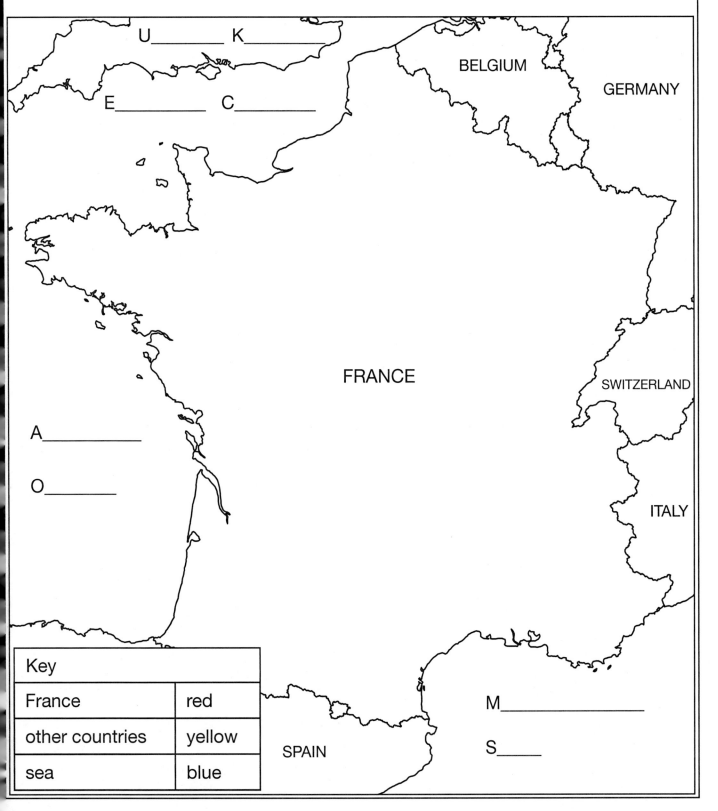

U_____ K_____

E_____ C_____

BELGIUM

GERMANY

FRANCE

SWITZERLAND

A_____

O_____

ITALY

M_____

Key	
France	red
other countries	yellow
sea	blue

S_____

SPAIN

23 Growing food

1. Fill in this survey of Parnac.

Landscape	
Is it an island?	
What is the name of the nearest river?	
Is the land flat or hilly?	
Climate	
Is it hot or cold, wet or dry?	
Are there any weather problems?	
Settlement	
Is it crowded or empty?	
What sort of buildings are there?	
Work	
How do people earn a living?	
What crops do farmers grow?	
What is made in Parnac?	
Tourism	
What would tourists like about Parnac and its surroundings?	

2. List four things in your own area that are different from Parnac.

a. ....

b. ....

c. ....

d. ....

24 Making cars

1. Colour each area of the car factory a different colour.

2. Complete the key using the same colours.

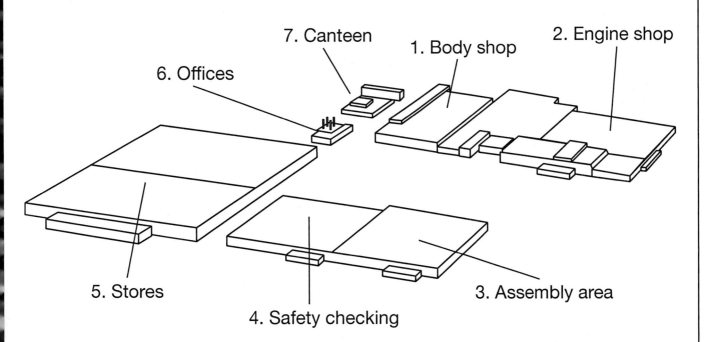

7. Canteen

1. Body shop

2. Engine shop

6. Offices

5. Stores

4. Safety checking

3. Assembly area

Area	Colour
1.	
2.	
3.	
4.	
5.	
6.	
7.	

3. Say which area of the factory these people would use.

Mechanic ....   Painter ....

Cook ....   Secretary ....

Storeman ....   Inspector ....

25 Introducing South America

Name ....

1. Draw the symbols from the key on the correct part of South America.

2. Write the names of the cities next to the dots.

3. Which region of South America would you most like to live in?

_____

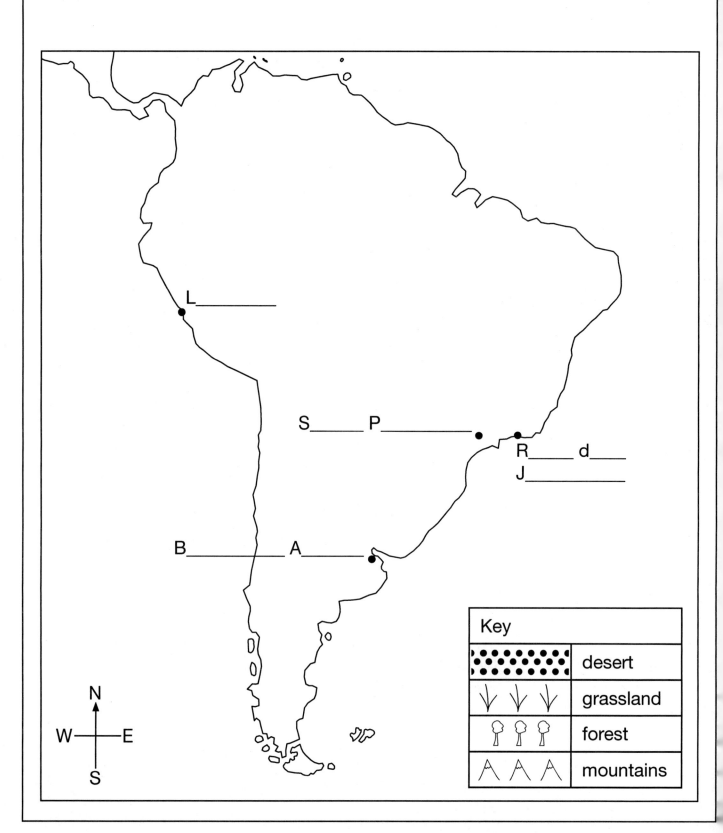

Key

(dots)	desert
↓ ↓ ↓	grassland
🌲 🌲 🌲	forest
Λ Λ Λ	mountains

1. Here are some objects from an exhibition about Chile.

Using the list label each picture.

map   volcanic lava   cloth   salmon   grapes   copper

2. In the empty boxes say why you think each object was chosen.

3. What six objects would you put in an exhibition about the UK?

....

....

....

Name ....

1. Draw pictures of the special Galapagos creatures in the empty boxes.

2. Join each picture to the correct symbol on the island.

3. Write the names of the island under each picture.

4. Colour the islands green and use blue around the coast.

Giant Tortoise	Sally Lightfoot Crab
Island	Island

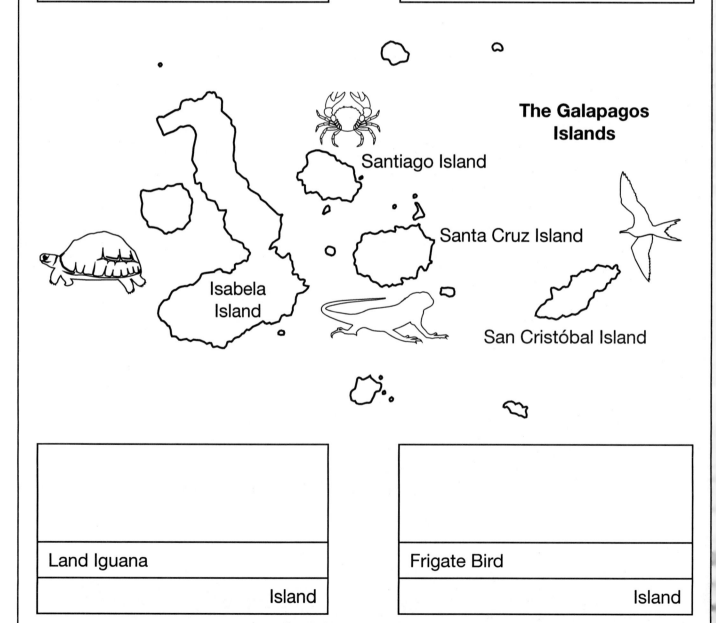

Santiago Island

The Galapagos Islands

Santa Cruz Island

Isabela Island

San Cristóbal Island

Land Iguana	Frigate Bird
Island	Island

Name ....

1. Colour in the symbols in the key.

2. Draw the symbols in the right places on the map.

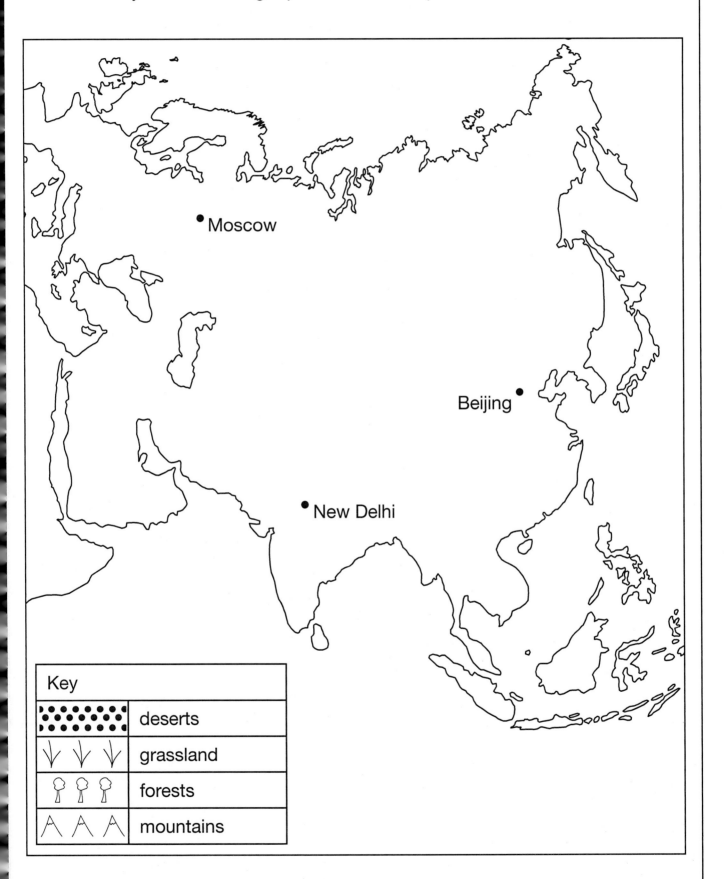

29 # India: A country in Asia   *Name* ....

1. Colour the map to show land and sea. Mark the capital city of India.

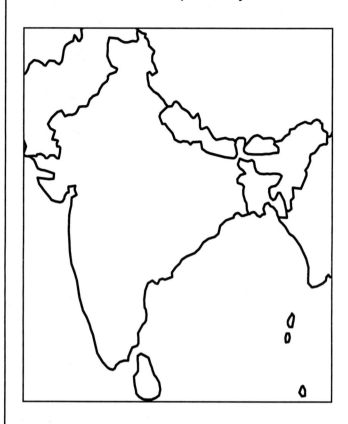

2. Colour the picture of the River Ganges and write a sentence underneath.

....

....

....

3. Complete the factfile below.

FACTFILE

Mountains   ....

Main river   ....

Population   ....

Two nearby   ....
countries
               ....

Flag

4. Use this space for a picture of India downloaded from the internet.

Name ....

1. Colour in the pictures.

2. Name the pictures using this list:

water tank   banyan tree   school   temple

3. Draw a line from each picture to the right place on the map.

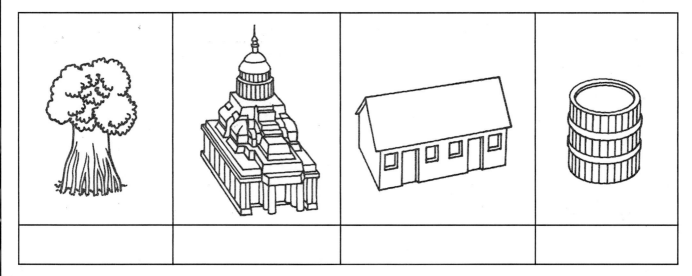

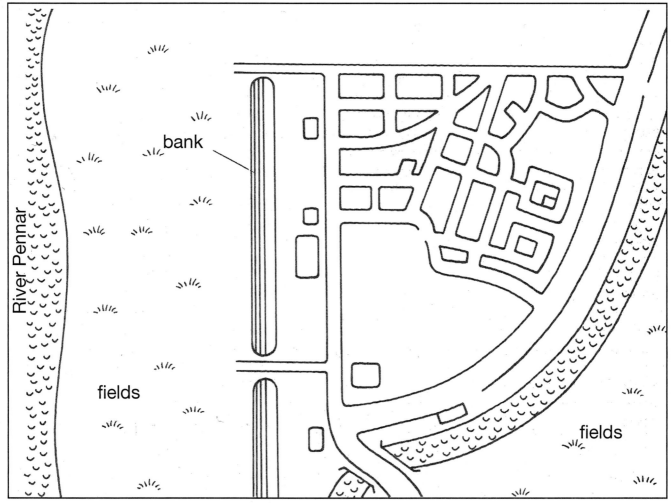

Geography in the English National Curriculum

A new primary geography curriculum was introduced in England in 2014. This new curriculum provides a framework for schools to follow but leaves teachers considerable scope to select and organise the content according to their individual needs. It should also be noted that the curriculum is only intended to occupy a proportion of the school day and that schools are free to devise their own studies in the time that remains.

Purpose of study

The aim of geographical education is clearly articulated in the opening section of the Programme of Study which states:

A high quality geography education should inspire in pupils a curiosity and fascination about the world and its people that will remain with them for the rest of their lives. Teaching should equip pupils with knowledge about diverse places, people, resources and natural and human environments, together with a deep understanding of the Earth's key physical and human processes. As pupils progress, their growing knowledge about the world should help them to deepen their understanding of the interaction between physical and human processes, and of the formation and use of landscapes and environments. Geographical knowledge, understanding and skills provide the frameworks and approaches that explain how the Earth's features at different scales are shaped and interconnected and change over time.

Subject content

The National Curriculum provides the following general guidance for each Key Stage:

Key Stage 1

Pupils should develop knowledge about the world, the United Kingdom and their locality. They should understand basic subject-specific vocabulary relating to human and physical geography and begin to use geographical skills, including first-hand observation, to enhance their locational awareness.

Key Stage 2

Pupils should extend their knowledge and understanding beyond the local area to include the United Kingdom and Europe, North and South America. This will include the location and characteristics of a range of the world's most significant human and physical features. They should develop their use of geographical knowledge, understanding and skills to enhance their locational and place knowledge.

Teachers who are familiar with the previous version of the curriculum will note the increasing emphasis on factual and place knowledge. For example, there is a greater focus on learning about the UK and Europe. Map reading and communication skills are also highlighted. On the other hand, there are no specific references to the developing world and sustainability is not mentioned directly. However, there is an expectation that schools will work from the Programmes of Study to develop a broad and balanced curriculum which meets the needs of learners in their locality. This provides schools with scope to enrich the curriculum and rectify any omissions which they may perceive.

Key Stage 2 Programme of study

The elements specified in the Key Stage 2 programme of study are listed below. The summary provided here should read alongside the statements about the wider aims of the curriculum. There is no suggestion that pupils should work to individual statements.

Focus
Extend knowledge of UK, Europe and North and South America
Location of world's most significant human and physical features
Knowledge, understanding and skills to enhance locational and place knowledge
Locational knowledge
Locate the world's countries
Use maps to focus on countries, cities and regions in Europe
Use maps to focus on countries, cities and regions in North America
Use maps to focus on countries, cities and regions in South America
Name and locate counties of the UK
Name and locate cities of the UK
Geographical regions of the UK
Topographical features of the UK
Changing land use patterns of the UK
Significance of latitude and longitude
Significance of Equator, Northern and Southern Hemisphere, Tropics of Cancer/Capricorn, Arctic/Antarctic circles, Prime Meridian
Time zones
Day and night
Place knowledge
Regional study within UK
Regional study in a European country
Regional study in North America
Regional study in South America
Human and physical geography
Climate zones
Biomes and vegetation belts
Rivers and mountains
Volcanoes and earthquakes
Water cycle
Types of settlement and land use
Economic activity including trade links
Distribution of natural resources including energy, food, minerals, water
Skills and fieldwork
Use maps, atlases, globes and digital mapping
Use eight points of the compass
Use four and six figure grid references
Use symbols and keys (including OS maps)
Fieldwork skills

WORLD MAP

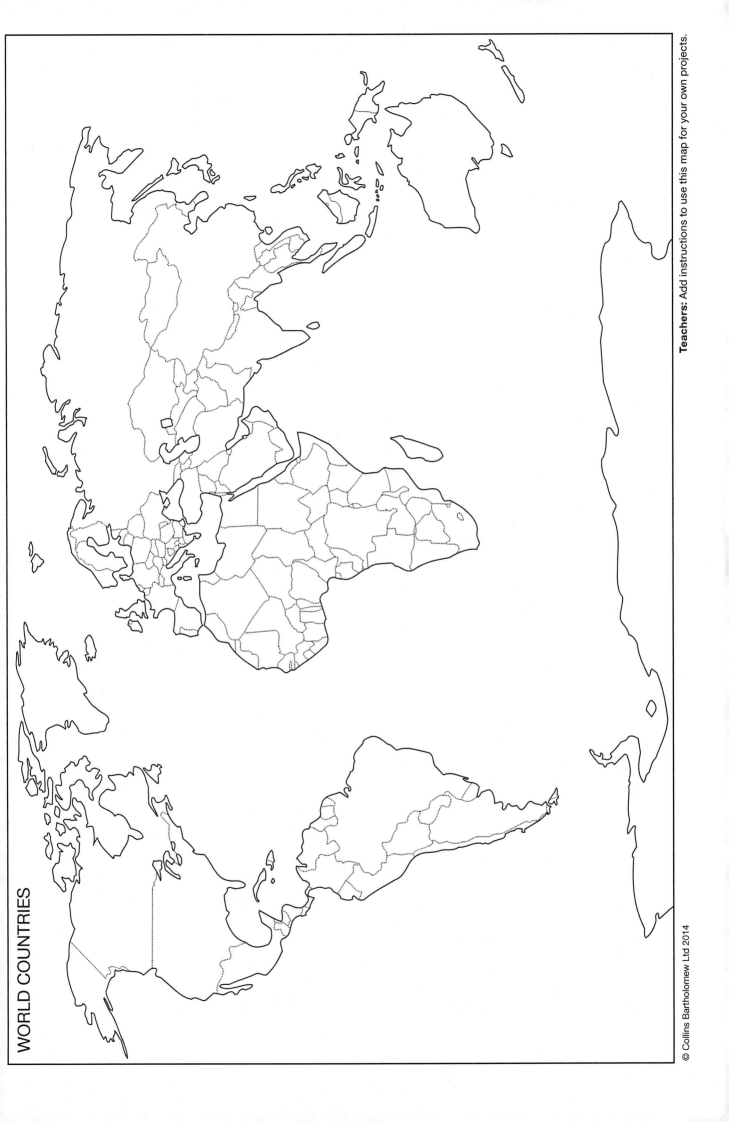

WORLD COUNTRIES

Primary Geography Teacher's Book 3
Collins
An imprint of HarperCollins Publishers
Westerhill Road
Bishopbriggs
Glasgow
G64 2QT

ISBN 978-0-00-756364-7

Imp 001

British Library Cataloguing in Publication Data
A catalogue record for this book is available from the British Library.

Printed by RR Donnelley at Glasgow, UK.

Acknowledgements

Additional original input by Terry Jewson

Cover designs Steve Evans illustration and design

Illustrations by Jouve Pvt Ltd pp 31, 34

Photo credits:

All images from www.shutterstock.com